Peterson Field Guides®
For Young Naturalists

Butterflies

Jonathan P. Latimer
Karen Stray Nolting

Illustrations by Amy Bartlett Wright

Foreword by Virginia Marie Peterson

Houghton Mifflin Company
Boston 2000

FOREWORD

My husband, Roger Tory Peterson, traced his interest in nature
back to an encounter he had with an exhausted flicker when he was
only 11 years old. When he found what he thought was a dead bird
in a bundle of brown feathers, he touched it and the bird suddenly exploded into life, showing its golden feathers. Roger said it was
"like resurrection." That experience was "the crucial moment"
that started Roger on a lifelong journey with nature. He combined
his passion for nature with his talent as an artist to create a series
of field guides and paintings that changed the way people experience the natural world. Roger often spoke of an even larger goal,
however. He believed that an understanding of the natural world
would lead people—especially young people—to a recognition of
"the interconnectedness of things all over the world." The Peterson Field Guides for Young Naturalists are a continuation of
Roger's interest in educating and inspiring young people to see
that "life itself is important—not just ourselves, but all life."

— *Virginia Marie Peterson*

Copyright © 2000 by Houghton Mifflin Company
Foreword copyright © 1999 by Virginia Marie Peterson
Illustrations copyright © 2000 by Amy Bartlett Wright
Illustrations from *A Field Guide to Western Butterflies* © 1999 by Amy Bartlett Wright and *Peterson First Guide to
Butterflies and Moths* © 1994 by Amy Bartlett Wright

The authors would like to thank Paul A. Opler, who reviewed and critiqued the manuscript, for his invaluable
suggestions. Thanks also to Paul E. Nolting for his continued support and encouragement.

Library of Congress Cataloging-in-Publication Data
Latimer, Jonathan P.
Butterflies / Jonathan P. Latimer, Karen Stray Nolting ; illustrations by Amy Bartlett Wright ; fore-
word by Virginia Marie Peterson.
p. cm.—(Peterson field guides for young naturalists)
Summary: A guide to help identify various butterflies, using the Peterson System of identification.
ISBN 0-395-97943-9.—ISBN 0-395-97944-7 (pbk.)
1. Butterflies Juvenile literature. [1. Butterflies.] I. Nolting, Karen Stray. II. Wright, Amy Bartlett,
ill. III. Title. IV Series.
QL544.2.L377   2000   595.78'9—dc21   99-38605   CIP

Photo credits
Black Swallowtail; Checkered White; Cabbage White; Clouded Sulphur; Orange Sulphur; Coral
Hairstreak; Gray Hairstreak; Eastern Tailed-Blue; Spring Azure; Variegated Fritillary; Mourning
Cloak; Red Admiral; Painted Lady; Viceroy; Common Wood-nymph; Monarch; Common Check-
ered-Skipper: Paul A. Opler. Eastern Tiger Swallowtail; Silver-spotted Skipper: Evi Buckner

Drawing on page 5 by Paul A. Opler from *A Field Guide to Eastern Butterflies*.
Copyright © 1992 by Paul A. Opler
Book design by Lisa Diercks. Typeset in Mrs Eaves and Base 9 from Emigre.
Manufactured in the United States of America
WOZ 10 9 8 7 6 5 4 3 2 1

CONTENTS

DISCOVERING BUTTERFLIES

Brightly colored butterflies floating in the breeze are a sure sign of warm weather. You may think their flight is carefree and aimless. You may also think butterflies look fragile and delicate as they move from flower to flower. But butterflies have complicated lives that are filled with surprises—and they are a lot tougher than you think!

This book will help you understand and identify some of the butterflies you are likely to see wherever you live in North America. It uses the method of identification invented by the man who revolutionized field guides, Roger Tory Peterson. He created a simple system of drawings and pointers (now known as the "Peterson System") that call attention to the unique marks on each kind of butterfly. It can help you answer the question *What kind of butterfly is that?*

What Kind of Butterfly Is That?

Figuring out what kind of butterfly you've seen is like solving a mystery. You gather clues and eventually you can find the answer. Here are some hints and questions you can ask when trying to identify an unknown butterfly.

Looking at a Butterfly Butterflies are insects, so they have six legs and their bodies are divided into three segments: the head, the thorax, and the abdomen. The head carries the butterfly's large eyes, its antennae, and a long tube for drinking, known as the *proboscis.* Butterflies use their proboscis like a straw to suck up liquids, such as nectar, water, and tree sap. They use their antennae for smelling, but the antennae have another important use.

Parts of a Butterfly

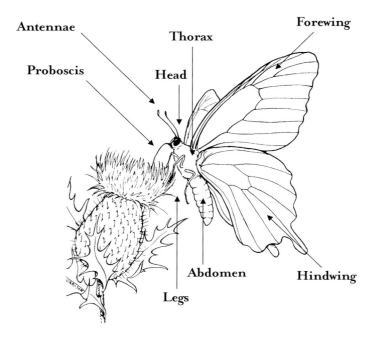

Antennae

Proboscis

Thorax

Head

Forewing

Abdomen

Legs

Hindwing

When a butterfly is flying, its antennae help it keep its balance.

To many of us, butterflies look as though they have only two wings. They actually have four—two on each side. The front wings are called *forewings* and the back wings are known as *hindwings*.

What Color Is the Butterfly? Butterflies are most easily identified by the colors on their wings. Each species has its own colors and markings, although there are usually variations in individual butterflies.

Does the Butterfly Have Any Marks? Many butterflies are marked with zigzags, spots, or bands. These marks break up the outline of a butterfly and make it harder for predators to see it.

Where Does a Butterfly's Color Come From?

You may notice that a butterfly sheds dust when it flies or if you touch it. This dust is made up of loose, powdery flakes, called *scales,* on its wings. These scales reflect light and give a butterfly its color.

A newly hatched butterfly may have more than a million scales on its wings. They are arranged in a neat pattern of overlapping rows, like shingles on a roof. But they start to fall off as soon as the butterfly begins flying. The wing underneath is actually transparent, like a wing of a housefly.

Eyespots—Some butterflies have spots on their wings that look like eyes. These eyespots can deceive predators in two ways. Large eyespots make the butterflies look like scary animals and may frighten predators away. Small eyespots may trick birds into striking the butterfly's tail rather than its head. Instead of a meal, the bird grabs a beakful of wing, which usually doesn't hurt the butterfly. Swallowtails and hairstreaks take this even further. Their tails resemble their heads and antennae. In some species the false head may be more noticeable than the real head.

Where Can You See Butterflies? Butterflies can be found almost anywhere, from meadows and forests to city parks and window boxes. In most cases, where you find them depends on where the food plants for their caterpillars grow. Butterflies visit plants to drink nectar and lay eggs. They also use plants for shelter from weather and to hide from predators.

Basking—Groups of butterflies often rest in sunny spots, especially early in the morning and on cloudy or cool days. Some may perch with their wings spread in order to absorb the sun's heat. Butterflies are cold-blooded, so they must get heat and energy from the sun. They move from place to place during the day to take advantage of the sunlight.

Puddling—Some butterflies also gather at wet or muddy spots on the ground. They drink the moisture and may get nourishment from the salts or minerals in the mud. Puddling butterflies may let you get very close to them.

Migration—Many butterflies spend their whole lives in a single field or meadow, but a few species, such as Monarchs and Painted Ladies, migrate long distances. This means that you may see unusual butterflies in your area, sometimes huge swarms of them.

The Life Cycle of a Butterfly One of the most amazing things about butterflies is their life cycle—the stages they pass through during their lives.

Egg—The first stage is spent as an egg. Eggs come in many shapes, but most are about the size of the head of a pin. Some hatch a few days after they are laid. Others wait through winter before hatching.

Butterfly eggs are often laid on the leaves or stems of a plant that will provide food for the caterpillar when it hatches. Adult female butterflies spend much time looking for the right plants for their eggs. Some lay their eggs one at a time; others lay them in clusters. Most females lay 100 or more eggs during their lifetime, but some lay many more.

Butterflies and Moths

What is the difference between a butterfly and a moth?

- Most butterflies fly during the day. Most moths do not.
- Butterflies are usually brightly colored. Moths are usually dull-colored.
- Butterflies have smooth, slender bodies. The bodies of moths tend to be rounded and fuzzy.
- Butterflies have knobbed antennae that look like clubs. Moths' antennae vary from straight threads to feathery or branched.

None of these differences are completely true all the time. Some moths look and act like butterflies and some butterflies look and act like moths.

Caterpillar—An egg hatches into a caterpillar, sometimes called a *larva.* Almost as soon as a caterpillar hatches, it starts eating. This is the stage when a butterfly does all its growing. Most caterpillars are very particular about the plants they eat, which are known as *host plants.* Many will only eat the leaves of one species.

In order to grow, a caterpillar must shed its skin. This is called *molting.* It usually happens four times during the caterpillar stage. Once a caterpillar is fully grown, it stops eating and begins looking for a place to go through its next stage. The caterpillar's skin splits one last time, revealing the *chrysalis.*

Chrysalis—A chrysalis, which is sometimes called a *pupa,* has a hard shell. It cannot crawl around or fly. Inside this hard shell a butterfly is forming. This process is known as *metamorphosis.* The butterfly that comes out of the chrysalis looks nothing like the caterpillar that it came from.

Butterfly—After several weeks or even months, the butterfly emerges. Its wings are shriveled from being inside the chrysalis. The butterfly expands its wings by pumping them full of fluid. After about an hour, it flies off.

The primary goal of a butterfly is to find a mate. They usually fly in sunshine, when they have the best chance of seeing a partner. The number of generations a butterfly has each year depends on its species. Some have one generation each year. Others, like the Cabbage White, have three or more.

Many butterflies live less than a week, but some, such as the Mourning Cloak, are known to live as long as 11 or 12 months. How long they live often depends on the weather, particularly for those that do not hibernate or migrate.

Keeping Track

Many people keep a list of all the butterflies they have ever seen. This is called a "Life List." You can begin yours with the list on page 48. It includes all the butterflies described in this book.

BLACK SWALLOWTAIL

Swallowtails include some of the most beautiful butter-flies found in North America. They are large—which makes them easy to see—and many of them have bright patterns on their wings. True to their name, Black Swallowtails are mostly black with yellow markings, but in the Far West individuals can be mostly yellow. Their double tails give them their name because they remind people of the tail of the swallow.

On warm afternoons male Black Swallowtails perch on shrubs, waiting for females. You may also find large numbers of male Black Swallowtails on hilltops or ridges because males tend to fly uphill. Although they are strong fliers, Black Swallowtails drift slowly from plant to plant as they feed. They also gather at puddles to drink.

Did You Know?

• As Black Swallowtail caterpillars feed, they store toxic chemicals from plants in their bodies. The bright color of an adult Swallowtail is a warning to birds that the butter-fly tastes bad and is poisonous.

• Adult Black Swallowtails are sometimes attracted to vegetables such as carrot and dill, so their caterpillars can be real pests in a garden.

• Black Swallowtails hibernate through winter as a chrysalis.

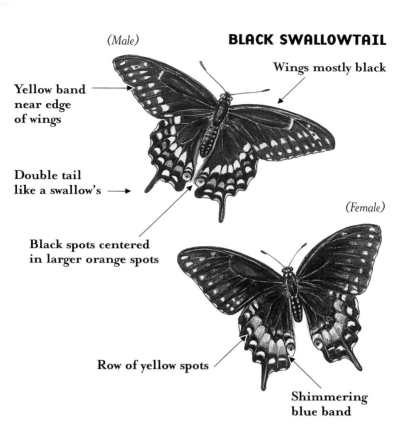

(Male)

BLACK SWALLOWTAIL

Wings mostly black

Yellow band
near edge
of wings

Double tail
like a swallow's →

(Female)

Black spots centered
in larger orange spots

Row of yellow spots

Shimmering
blue band

Habitat Swallowtails are found in a variety of open areas, including fields, suburbs, marshes, deserts, and roadsides throughout most of the eastern United States, southern Canada, and west to Colorado and southern California.

Favorite Plants Adults feed on nectar from flowers, including red clover, milkweed, and thistles. Caterpillars eat leaves of plants in the parsley family, including Queen Anne's Lace, carrot, celery, and dill, and sometimes plants in the citrus family.

When to See Them Black Swallowtails can be seen from April to October.

TIGER SWALLOWTAILS

Tiger Swallowtail caterpillars often feed in the tops of trees. Unfortunately, predators such as birds are also found in treetops. So the caterpillars of Tiger Swallowtails have developed an unusual way to avoid them. They make a shelter to hide in by curling leaves and tying them with their silk. Then they eat or rest on silken mats inside the curled leaves where birds are less likely to notice them.

Eastern Tiger Swallowtails can be seen in eastern North America from Canada to the Gulf of Mexico and as far west as Colorado and central Texas. Western Tiger Swallowtails are found from British Columbia to southern New Mexico and Baja California. They look similar, but they seldom stray into each other's territory.

Did You Know?

• Swallowtails get their name from the tails on their hindwings, which look like the V-shaped tail of a Barn Swallow.

• In 1587 a member of Sir Walter Raleigh's colony at Roanoke Island included a drawing of an Eastern Tiger Swallowtail in his report home.

• Tiger Swallowtails spend winter hibernating as a chrysalis. Their green or brown chrysalis may hang from a twig or tree bark.

• The Tiger Swallowtail is the state butterfly of Georgia, Ohio, Virginia, and Wyoming.

Eastern Tiger Swallowtail

TIGER SWALLOWTAILS

Yellow form— either male or female

Yellow with black stripes like a tiger's

Tail like a swallow's

Black with shadows of dark stripes

Yellow band near edge of wings

Black form— female only

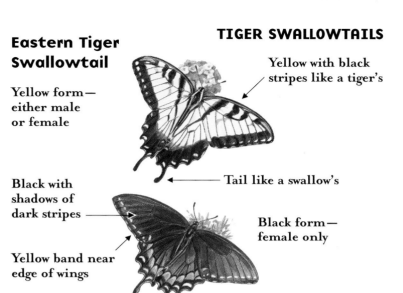

Western Tiger Swallowtail

Males and females look alike.

Narrower wings than the Eastern Tiger Swallowtail's

Habitat Tiger Swallowtails can be found in woods and parks and along forest edges and roadsides.

Favorite Plants Tiger Swallowtail caterpillars eat the leaves of various plants and trees, including cherry and cottonwood. Adult butterflies sip nectar from flowers.

When to See Them Eastern Tiger Swallowtails can be seen from February to November in the Deep South and from May to September in the North. Western Tiger Swallowtails can be found in June and July, but fly throughout much of the year in California.

CHECKERED WHITE

You can tell a Checkered White by its zigzag flight. It flies rapidly near the ground. Males can often be seen patrolling open fields or hilltops in the afternoon, looking for females.

Like many insects, Checkered White butterflies can see ultraviolet light. To our eyes, male and female Checkered Whites look similar, but in ultraviolet light they are easy to tell apart. The wing pattern of a male Checkered White butterfly absorbs ultraviolet light. The wing pattern of a female reflects it.

The population of Checkered Whites fluctuates from year to year. Large numbers can be seen one year and very few the next. Checkered White butterflies are known to travel miles to find their food plants.

Did You Know?
• The life span of an adult Checkered White butterfly is only about a week long.
• Checkered Whites hibernate through winter as a chrysalis.

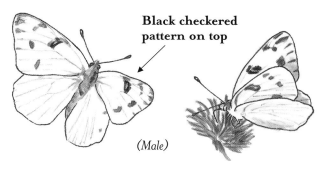

Black checkered
pattern on top

Markings on underside
of wings are paler.

(Male)

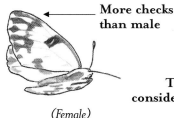

More checks
than male

The pattern of checks varies
considerably between individuals.

(Female)

Habitat Checkered Whites are found in dry areas in vacant lots, pastures, or along railroad tracks and roads. They can be found all year in the southern United States and northern Mexico. During the warm months they spread as far north as southern Canada but not to New England.

Favorite Plants Checkered White caterpillars eat buds, flowers, and fruits of plants in the mustard family. Adult butterflies sip nectar from mustard flowers and alfalfa.

When to See Them Checkered Whites can be seen from March to November in the North and throughout the year in the southern United States and northern Mexico.

CABBAGE WHITE

Cabbage Whites are one of the most common butterflies in North America. They appear early in spring and stay around until late summer. You may have seen them fluttering around the yard or garden, sipping flower nectar. They seem to prefer purple, blue, or yellow flowers. They also sip water from mud puddles.

You can often see males patrolling for females along the edges of woods or near their host plants. Their flight is lazy and wandering. When a male finds a possible mate, he flies erratically up and down in front of her until she lands. Then he lands beside her and flutters his wings. In farm areas females can be seen flying around cabbage plants, where they lay their eggs.

Did You Know?
• Cabbage Whites may be the most common butterfly in North America, but they are not natives. They were introduced to Quebec, Canada, from Eurasia in the 1860s.
• Cabbage White caterpillars can be a pest on cabbages, broccoli, and kale.

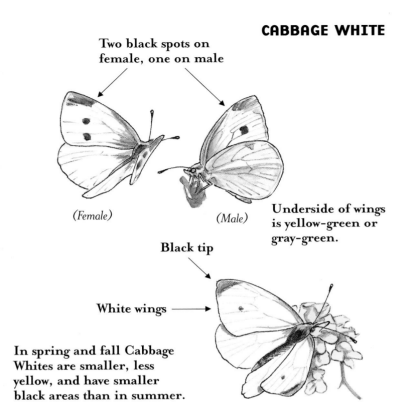

Two black spots on
female, one on male

(Female)   (Male)

Underside of wings
is yellow-green or
gray-green.

Black tip

White wings

In spring and fall Cabbage
Whites are smaller, less
yellow, and have smaller
black areas than in summer.

Habitat Cabbage Whites live in almost any type of open
space, including weedy areas, gardens, roadsides, cities,
and suburbs. They are found throughout the United
States and central Canada.

Favorite Plants Cabbage White Caterpillars have been
found eating more than 80 different kinds of plants, but
they are most often found on plants in the mustard family, especially cabbage. Adults sip flower nectar from a very
wide array of plants, including mustards, dandelions,
nasturtiums, red clover, asters, and mints.

When to See Them The Cabbage White is usually the
first butterfly to emerge in spring.

CLOUDED SULPHUR

O n bright days large numbers of Clouded Sulphurs can be seen fluttering over open fields. Males fly in spirals, rising high into the air as part of their courtship dance. A butterfly's main task is to mate, and Clouded Sulphurs must hurry because many of them live for only a few days.

Most butterfly species have developed their own pattern of courtship. They have their own timing, their own habitat, and their own set of behaviors. Mating between species is a rare thing. Under crowded conditions, however, Clouded Sulphurs mate with their close relatives, Orange Sulphurs. Their offspring have part-orange and part-yellow wings. This can sometimes make identifying these butterflies confusing.

Did You Know?

- Adult Clouded Sulphurs are often found near plants with yellow flowers.
- In spring and fall Clouded Sulphurs are smaller and less clearly marked.
- The Clouded Sulphur is sometimes called the Common Sulphur.

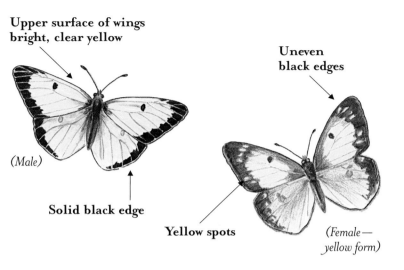

Upper surface of wings bright, clear yellow

Uneven black edges

(Male)

Solid black edge

Yellow spots

(Female— yellow form)

There are two female forms— a yellow form and a white form. White form of female is greenish white rather than yellow.

Habitat Clouded Sulphurs can be found throughout the United States except for much of California, south Texas, and most of Florida. They range as far north as Alaska and most of Canada. They can be seen in many different open areas, including fields, lawns, alfalfa and clover fields, road edges, and meadows.

Favorite Plants Adult Clouded Sulphurs sip flower nectar from many plants. Clouded Sulphur caterpillars can be found on plants in the Pea family, including alfalfa and white clover.

When to See Them Clouded Sulphurs can be seen from May to October in the North and from March to November in the South.

ORANGE SULPHUR

Orange Sulphurs can often be seen flying over fields of alfalfa or clover with their close relatives, Clouded Sulphurs. When you find them together, any butterfly that has orange on its wings is considered an Orange Sulphur. Otherwise, it's a Clouded Sulphur.

Orange Sulphurs have spread across North America. They are one of the most successful butterflies, although their caterpillars are sometimes considered pests.

You can tell when Orange Sulphur caterpillars have been feeding by looking closely at the leaves of clover or alfalfa. Young caterpillars chew holes in the tops of leaves, then eat the leaf from the tip down. Older caterpillars eat one half of a leaf first, then the other half.

Did You Know?

- The Orange Sulphur is one of the most widespread and common butterflies in North America.
- The Orange Sulphur caterpillar can be an occasional pest in alfalfa fields, which is why it is sometimes called the Alfalfa Butterfly.

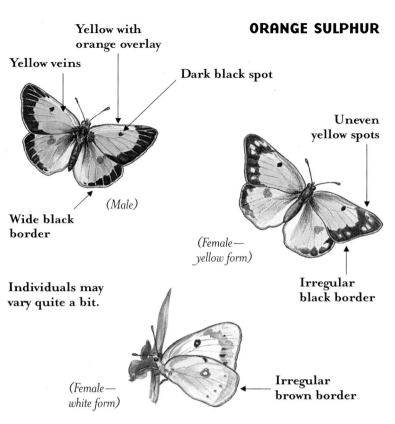

Yellow with orange overlay

Yellow veins

Dark black spot

Uneven yellow spots

(Male)

Wide black border

(Female — yellow form)

Individuals may vary quite a bit.

Irregular black border

(Female — white form)

Irregular brown border

Habitat Orange Sulphurs can be found in a wide variety of open sites, especially in clover or alfalfa fields, vacant lots, meadows, and along the edges of roads. Orange Sulphurs range from coast to coast in the United States, except for Florida.

Favorite Plants Orange Sulphur caterpillars can be found on alfalfa, white clover, and white sweet clover. Adults sip nectar from many kinds of flowers, including dandelions, milkweeds, goldenrods, and asters.

When to See Them Orange Sulphurs can be seen from June to October in the North and from March to November in the South.

CORAL HAIRSTREAK

During the day Coral Hairstreak caterpillars hide from predators in the dead leaves at the base of their food plants. Coral Hairstreak caterpillars have developed another defense that is even stranger—they use ants for protection.

Coral Hairstreak caterpillars "bribe" ants by producing a sweet liquid called honeydew. In repayment, the ants protect the caterpillars from predators such as beetles and wasps. But there is also danger in this deal. Ants will attack almost anything that moves, so Coral Hairstreak caterpillars must stay very still while the ants are around. At night the ants rest in their colony underground. The caterpillars can then move around safely and feed on leaves.

Did You Know?
• These little butterflies are swift fliers, but they usually linger around their favorite host plants.

• Male Coral hairstreaks perch on shrubs to watch for females, especially in the late afternoon. They sometimes investigate other males or other flying insects that pass by.

• Female Coral Hairstreaks lay their eggs one at a time on twigs or in the litter at the base of a food plant. The eggs hibernate through winter.

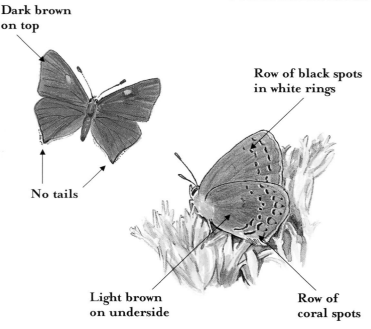

Dark brown
on top

Row of black spots
in white rings

No tails

Light brown
on underside

Row of
coral spots

Males have pointed, triangular wings.
Females have rounded hindwings.

Habitat Coral Hairstreak butterflies can be found in shrubby areas, open woodlands, pastures, and along streams. They range from Canada and New England south to California, Texas, and central Georgia.

Favorite Plants Adult Coral Hairstreaks sip nectar from flowers, including butterflyweed, New Jersey tea, sulphur flower, and bee plant. Coral Hairstreak caterpillars eat the leaves and fruit of wild cherry, wild plum, chokecherry, and some other members of the Rose family.

When to See Them Coral Hairstreaks can be seen from May to August.

GRAY HAIRSTREAK

Gray Hairstreaks are one of many butterflies that have developed a special way to fool predators. They have hairlike tails that stick out from the back of their wings. When Gray Hairstreaks perch, these tails look like the antennae on the head of a butterfly. Gray Hairstreaks

also have bright red-orange spots on their wings that look like eyes. These eyespots and the false antennae are often enough to trick a bird into attacking the wrong end of the butterfly. You may see a Gray Hairstreak or other butterfly that has lost part of its tail, but the butterfly gets along fine without it.

A Gray Hairstreak adds to its disguise by perching with its head pointed downward. This is the opposite direction from most other butterflies.

Did You Know?

• Hairstreaks get their name from their short, threadlike tails. The Gray Hairstreak is the most widespread hairstreak in North America.

• The Gray Hairstreak caterpillar sometimes damages bean and cotton crops. It is known as the Cotton Borer in some places because young caterpillars feed on flowers and fruits by boring into them.

• Gray Hairstreaks hibernate through winter as a chrysalis.

GRAY HAIRSTREAK

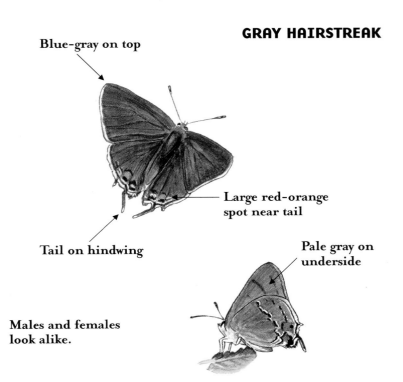

Blue-gray on top

Large red-orange spot near tail

Tail on hindwing

Pale gray on underside

Males and females look alike.

Underside is dark gray in spring and fall, but it is paler gray in summer.

Habitat Gray Hairstreaks can be seen in open areas, especially in weedy fields. They range throughout the United States from southern Canada to Mexico.

Favorite Plants Gray Hairstreak caterpillars can be found on the flowers and fruits of an almost endless variety of plants, including beans, clovers, cotton, and mallows. Adults sip nectar from many flowering plants, including milkweed, mint, goldenrod, and white sweet clover.

When to See Them Gray Hairstreaks can be seen from May to September in the North and from February to November in the South.

TAILED-BLUES

Even with their wings fully spread, these tiny butterflies are a little less than an inch across. They call attention to themselves when they drink nectar because they usually rub their hindwings back and forth. When the sun strikes a male's shimmering blue wings, they sparkle like jewels. Females are mainly brown, but their color varies with the season. In spring they have blue at the base of their wings. Western Tailed-Blues are often a little larger than Eastern Tailed-Blues, but they look very similar. Tailed-Blues are the only blue species with a hairlike tail on each hindwing.

Like many butterflies, both Tailed-Blues gather at mud puddles. Aside from drinking water, some experts think that they obtain valuable salts and minerals from the mud.

Did You Know?
- Tailed-Blues tend to live their whole lives in a small area.
- Tailed-Blue caterpillars hibernate through winter, often in the seed pods of one of their food plants. Early in spring they form a chrysalis and become an adult butterfly.
- Although most other Blues perch with their wings closed, Eastern Tailed-Blues sometimes bask with their wings half open.

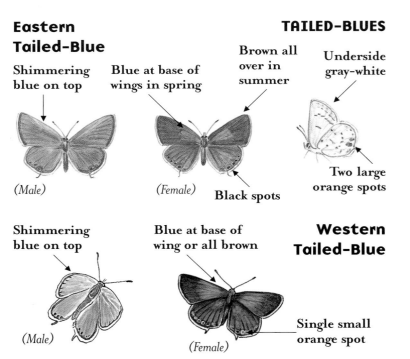

Eastern
Tailed-Blue

TAILED-BLUES

Shimmering blue on top

Blue at base of wings in spring

Brown all over in summer

Underside gray-white

(Male)

(Female)

Black spots

Two large orange spots

Shimmering blue on top

Blue at base of wing or all brown

Western
Tailed-Blue

(Male)

(Female)

Single small orange spot

Habitat Eastern Tailed-Blues are found in open, sunny places from southeast Canada and the eastern United States to southeastern Arizona. They are also abundant in the central valley of California. Western Tailed-Blues can be seen in open areas with low shrubs and in meadows from Alaska to northern Mexico.

Favorite Plants Eastern Tailed-Blue caterpillars can be found on plants in the Pea family, including alfalfa and clover. Western Tailed-Blue caterpillars can be found on false lupine and vetches. Adults sip nectar from many flowers.

When to See Them Eastern Tailed-Blues can be seen from April to November in the North and from February to November in the South. Western Tailed-Blues appear from March to July.

SPRING AZURE

These small blue butterflies appear almost as soon as the weather begins to warm in spring. Male Spring Azures patrol and perch all day, looking for females, but they are most active from late afternoon until dusk. They fly about 3 feet above the ground and often gather at wet soil on roads or near streams.

Adult Spring Azures also flutter higher up near flowers on trees, especially dogwood and viburnum. They drink nectar from these flowers, and females lay their eggs on flower buds. Spring Azure caterpillars feed on flowers and fruits and are protected by ants. Like Coral Hairstreak caterpillars, Spring Azure caterpillars "bribe" ants to look after them by producing honeydew.

Did You Know?
- Spring Azures are often the first butterfly you will see in spring. Later in the year they are joined by Summer Azures, which look similar.
- Spring Azures hibernate through winter as a chrysalis.

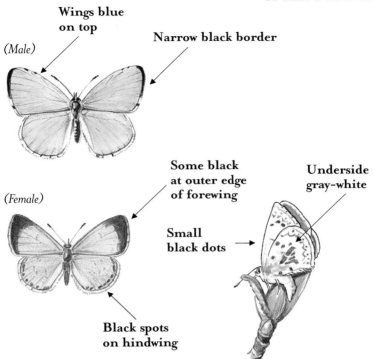

Wings blue on top

Narrow black border

(Male)

Some black at outer edge of forewing

(Female)

Underside gray-white

Small black dots

Black spots on hindwing

Habitat Spring Azures can be found in clearings, along the edges of woods, and in freshwater marshes and swamps. They range as far north as Alaska and Canada, and through most of the United States, except the Texas coast, the southern plains, and Florida.

Favorite Plants Caterpillars eat the flowers of a variety of shrubs and trees, especially ones with clusters of flowers, such as dogwood and cherry. Adults sip flower nectar from dogbane, privet, blackberry, common milkweed, and many others.

When to See Them Spring Azures can be found from January to May along the Gulf Coast and from May to August in Canada.

VARIEGATED FRITILLARY

The orange wings of a Variegated Fritillary are marked with an amazingly complex pattern of black lines and spots, which gives this butterfly its name. These butterflies can often be seen flying close to the ground or fluttering their wings when they stop at flowers. Violets are a favorite food of Variegated Fritillaries, but they will also visit a variety of other plants.

The caterpillar and chrysalis of a Variegated Fritillary are among the most beautiful in North America. The caterpillar is white with 5 red bands that run from head to tail. Bunches of black spines stick out of the white areas. Its head is red and has 2 long black spines. The chrysalis is a shiny pale green with gold bumps and black, yellow, and orange markings.

Did You Know?

• Variegated Fritillaries cannot survive northern winters. They spread northward from the South each spring.

• Fritillaries get their name from the spots on their wings, which look like dots on dice. The word fritillary comes from a Latin word for dice-box.

VARIEGATED FRITILLARY

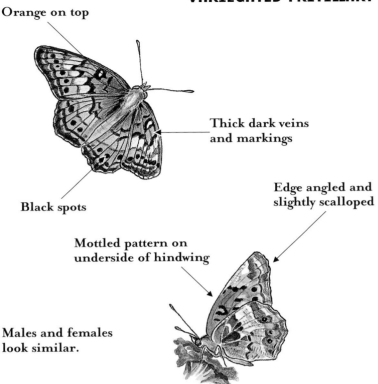

Orange on top

Thick dark veins
and markings

Black spots

Edge angled and
slightly scalloped

Mottled pattern on
underside of hindwing

Males and females
look similar.

Habitat Variegated Fritillaries can be seen in open, sunny areas such as prairies, fields, pastures, road edges, and landfills. They are regularly found throughout most of the United States except the Pacific Northwest.

Favorite Plants Variegated Fritillary caterpillars eat a variety of plants, including violets, passionflowers, pansies, and stonecrop. Adults sip nectar from butterflyweed, common milkweed, peppermint, red clover, and sunflower.

When to See Them Variegated Fritillaries can be seen from April to October in the North and from February or March to November or December in the South.

MOURNING CLOAK

Mourning Cloaks are one of the few butterflies that hibernate through winter as an adult butterfly. Most butterflies spend winter as an egg, caterpillar, or hibernating as a chrysalis. Mourning Cloaks find shelter in a wood pile, behind loose bark, or even in the eaves of a house. Because of this, Mourning Cloaks are often the first butterflies seen in spring. When the temperature reaches about 60 degrees, they start to fly around, searching for nectar or other foods. They often go to holes made by woodpeckers to sip the oozing sap.

Several Mourning Cloak caterpillars live together in a web and feed on young leaves. Adults emerge in June or July. After feeding briefly, the adults go into a dormant state until fall. Then they reemerge to feed and store energy for hibernation.

Did You Know?

- An adult Mourning Cloak may have the longest life of any butterfly in North America. They can live for 11 to 12 months.
- Mourning Cloak butterflies walk down a tree trunk to find sap. They feed with their head pointed downward.
- Mourning Cloak butterflies bask with their wings open in the afternoon. When it becomes too hot, they perch in the shade with their wings closed.

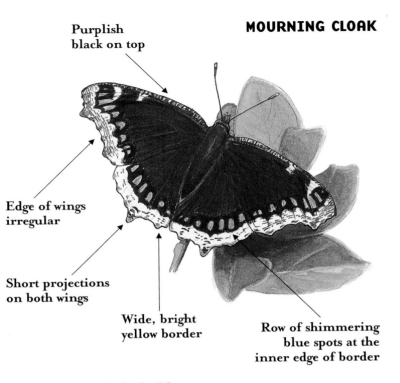

Purplish
black on top

Edge of wings
irregular

Short projections
on both wings

Wide, bright
yellow border

Row of shimmering
blue spots at the
inner edge of border

Males and females look alike.

Habitat Mourning Cloaks are found almost anywhere that host plants occur, including woods, parks, and suburbs. They range throughout all of North America south to central Mexico. They are found less often in the Gulf states and Florida.

Favorite Plants Mourning Cloak caterpillars can be found on black willow and weeping willow and on American elm, cottonwood, aspen, paper birch, and hackberry. Adult Mourning Cloaks eat tree sap. They also feed on rotting fruit and flower nectar.

When to See Them Mourning Cloaks can be seen throughout most of the year.

RED ADMIRAL

I f you find a Red Admiral, you may be able to see it again in the same place for several days or even weeks at a time. When they find a spot, male Red Admirals usually stay a while. They can often be seen along a hedge or line of brush or on a hilltop. They perch in a sunny place mainly in the afternoon or evening. When other males or females approach, they fly out to confront them. Male Red Admirals are even known to chase after birds. Their flight is erratic and rapid.

Sometimes you can get close to their perch without disturbing a Red Admiral. Some will fly out to investigate you—and they might even land on you.

Did You Know?

• Red Admirals cannot survive where it freezes in winter. Each spring they must migrate from the South across most of North America. Where the weather is milder, Red Admiral butterflies sometimes hibernate through winter.
• Young Red Admiral caterpillars eat and live within a shelter made from folded leaves. Older caterpillars make a nest by tying leaves together with silk.

RED ADMIRAL

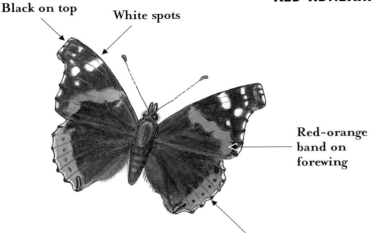

Black on top

White spots

Red-orange band on forewing

Red-orange band on edge of hindwing

The Red Admirals you see in summer are larger and brighter than the ones you see in winter.

Males and females look alike.

Habitat Red Admirals can be found in woods, yards, parks, marshes, and moist fields. During migrations, they can be found in almost any habitat. They range from Central America and Mexico throughout the United States to northern Canada and southern Alaska.

Favorite Plants Red Admiral butterflies drink sap from trees and rotting fruit. They visit flowers, such as common milkweed, red clover, and aster, only when other sources of food are not available. Caterpillars eat plants in the Nettle family.

When to See Them Red Admirals can be seen from March to October in most of North America. From October to March they can be found in southern Texas and Mexico.

PAINTED LADY

Every few years a great northward migration begins in spring in the deserts of northern Mexico. Millions of Painted Lady butterflies fly northward, traveling hundreds of miles. They can be found everywhere, except the Far North. Even the ocean doesn't stop them. Swarms of Painted Ladies have been seen far out at sea.

Next to the Monarch, the Painted Lady is the most amazing migratory butterfly in North America, but there is a difference. Painted Ladies usually migrate only one way. The cold weather kills off the Painted Ladies in the North, and Painted Ladies from the South must recolonize the continent each year. Except in the deserts of the Southwest, the Painted Ladies you see are recent arrivals.

Did You Know?

- The Painted Lady is sometimes known as the Thistle Butterfly because of its caterpillar's appetite for thistle.
- The Painted Lady is also called the Cosmopolitan because it is the most widespread butterfly in the world. It is found on all continents except Australia and Antarctica.
- Painted Ladies fly straight and fast, but they sometimes dance erratically in the air.

Black patch

White bar

Orange-pink

Row of 4 small black spots

Darker at base of wing

Black, brown, and gray pattern on underside

Four small eyespots

Males and females look alike.

Habitat Painted Ladies can be found in open areas almost anywhere, including gardens. They migrate from the deserts of northern Mexico throughout the United States and Canada south of the Arctic.

Favorite Plants Painted Lady caterpillars have been found on more than 100 different kinds of plants but most often on thistles and mallows. Adults prefer nectar from plants that grow 3 to 6 feet high, especially thistles, asters, and ironweed. They also visit red clover, privet, milkweeds, black-eyed Susan, and sunflowers.

When to See Them Painted Ladies can be seen from May to October in the East and from October to April in the Southwest and California.

VICEROY

The Viceroy looks like the twin of the Monarch butterfly. This is known as mimicry. Mimicry is used as a

defense against predators by a number of butterflies. Their markings look like species that taste bad to predators. Many bad-tasting butterflies have boldly colored wings that warn predators to beware. Once a predator gets a taste of one of these butterflies, it is unlikely to go after anything that looks like it again. A Viceroy fools predators by mimicking the bright orange and black markings of a Monarch.

Young Viceroy caterpillars make a ball out of bits of leaves and silk that hang off the leaf they are eating. It is suspected the ball may divert predators and keep them from attacking the caterpillar. Older caterpillars spend winter in a shelter made from a rolled leaf.

Did You Know?
- You can tell a Viceroy from a Monarch by its smaller size and the way it holds its wings when it rests. The wings of a Viceroy are held partly open. A Monarch closes its wings. Monarchs are also steady fliers. A Viceroy makes a few quick beats with its wings, then glides, then beats again.
- In Florida, Georgia, and the Southwest where Monarchs are rare, Viceroys are brown instead of orange.
- The Viceroy butterfly is the official state insect of Kansas and Kentucky.

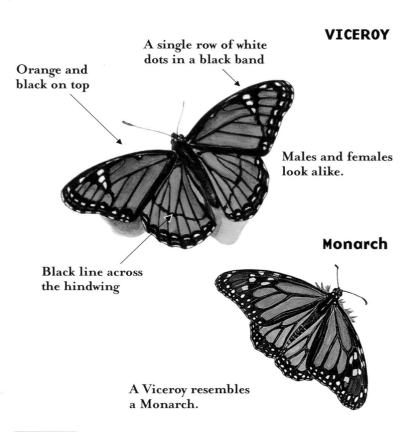

VICEROY

A single row of white
dots in a black band

Orange and
black on top

Males and females
look alike.

Monarch

Black line across
the hindwing

A Viceroy resembles
a Monarch.

Habitat Viceroys can be seen in wet areas, such as the edges of lakes or swamps, in willow groves, wet meadows, and along roadsides. They range from the Atlantic Coast to the eastern edges of the Cascade and Sierra Nevada mountains.

Favorite Plants Viceroy caterpillars can be found on willows, poplars, and cottonwoods. Adult butterflies feed on nectar from flowers, such as asters and goldenrods, and on rotting fruit.

When to See Them Viceroys can be found from May to September throughout most of their range, except in Florida, where they can be seen all year.

COMMON WOOD-NYMPH

Common Wood-nymphs are sometimes hard to identify because they look so different from place to place. Common Wood-nymphs that live in the South or along the coast are larger than Wood-nymphs that live inland. They also have a yellow or yellow-orange patch on their forewing. Wood-nymphs that live inland have either a smaller yellow patch or no patch at all, but they all have one unique mark—the 2 eyespots on their forewings.

Eyespots are a special form of defense against predators. When a butterfly is startled, it will suddenly spread its wings and display its eyespots. This often distracts a bird or even scares it away. It has been suggested that the eyespots remind birds of the eyes of a snake.

Did You Know?
• Male Common Wood-nymphs patrol grassy areas with an irregular, jumpy flight, looking for females. Females are less active and often rest in the shade.
• Common Wood-nymph caterpillars hatch but do not feed. Instead they hibernate until spring. Females emerge later than males.
• The Common Wood-nymph is also known as the Large Wood-nymph, the Goggle Eye, or the Blue-eyed Grayling.

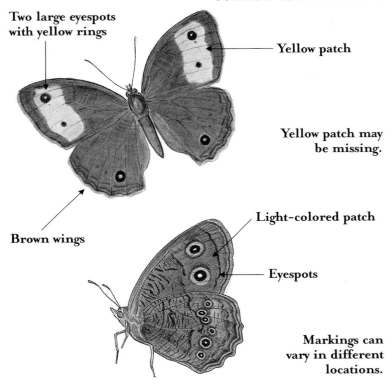

Two large eyespots with yellow rings

Yellow patch

Yellow patch may be missing.

Brown wings

Light-colored patch

Eyespots

Markings can vary in different locations.

Males and females look similar.

Habitat Common Wood-nymphs can be found throughout southern Canada and the United States, except for the Southwest, southern Florida, and northern Maine. They can be seen in sunny, grassy areas, including prairies, open meadows, marshes, and fields.

Favorite Plants Common Wood-nymph caterpillars can be found on grasses. Adults feed very little, but sometimes eat rotting fruit or flower nectar.

When to See Them Common Wood-nymph butterflies can be seen from late May to October.

MONARCH

The Monarch is the long-distance champion among butterflies. From August to October, huge numbers of Monarchs migrate south, flying thousands of miles to hibernate along the California coast or in the mountains of central Mexico. They stop along the way to feed on nectar and to roost together at night. Millions, perhaps even billions, of butterflies gather at the wintering sites in Mexico, covering the trees with their bright orange wings.

In spring individual Monarchs fly north by themselves. Along the way, females lay eggs and then die. It takes two

generations to reach the northern United States and southern Canada by June. Throughout summer adults lay more eggs. In late summer these eggs produce the generation of Monarchs that will return south in fall.

Did You Know?
• Monarch caterpillars eat milkweed plants, which make them and their butterflies taste very bad. Their bright color warns birds not to eat them.
• Monarchs have flown across the Atlantic from North America and have been found in Europe.
• Work is under way to protect all the sites in California and Mexico where Monarchs winter.
• The Monarch is the state butterfly of Alabama, Illinois, and Vermont.

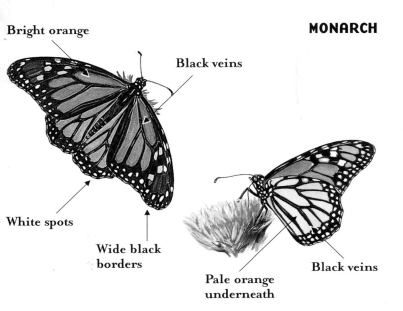

Bright orange

Black veins

White spots

Wide black borders

Pale orange underneath

Black veins

Females are duller colored than males, and the black veins on their wings are blurry and thicker.

Habitat Monarchs can be found in almost any open area. They range from southern Canada through all of the United States, Central America, and most of South America. They are also found in Australia, Hawaii, and other Pacific Islands.

Favorite Plants Monarch caterpillars can be found on most kinds of milkweeds. Adult Monarchs sip nectar from the flowers of all milkweeds. Early in the season before milkweeds bloom, they visit a variety of flowers. As milkweeds begin to fade in fall, adult Monarchs visit goldenrods and other flowers.

When to See Them Monarchs can be found through-out North America during spring and summer. They may be seen all year in Florida, southern Texas, and southeastern California.

SILVER-SPOTTED SKIPPER

Silver-spotted Skippers are often found where people live. They can be seen in gardens, parks, and suburban neighborhoods. Their gold spots and silver bands make them unmistakable. They become even more obvious when they fly out to inspect anything that happens to pass by.

On sunny mornings male Silver-spotted Skippers

perch on branches or tall weeds, waiting for females. When a female appears, several males may fly out and pursue her. They are vigorous fliers, and sometimes they put on amazing aerial displays. In the afternoon males often hang upside-down under leaves.

Did You Know?
• Skippers get their name from their swift, powerful flight, which looks like a stone skipping across water. They are usually faster than other butterflies but fly shorter distances.
• Only a few skippers migrate. Most hibernate through winter as a chrysalis or a caterpillar.
• Silver-spotted Skippers almost never visit yellow flowers. They favor blue, red, pink, purple, and sometimes white or cream-colored ones.

SILVER-SPOTTED SKIPPER

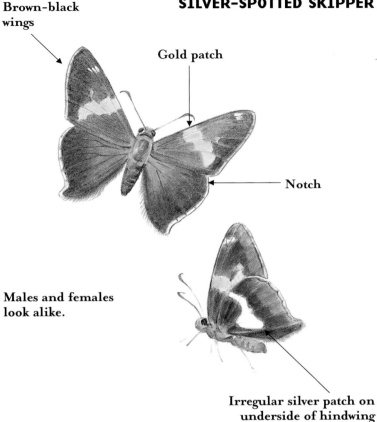

Brown-black
wings

Gold patch

Notch

Males and females
look alike.

Irregular silver patch on
underside of hindwing

Habitat Silver-spotted Skippers can be found near
locust trees in open woods and on prairies or along
streams and waterways from southern Canada to northern Mexico.

Favorite Plants Silver-spotted Skipper caterpillars are
found on locust trees and wisteria. Adults sip nectar from
common milkweed, red clover, and thistles.

When to See Them Silver-spotted Skippers can be
seen from May to September in most of the North and
West and from February to December in the Deep South.

COMMON CHECKERED-SKIPPER

Common Checkered-Skippers look like whirring blue blurs when they fly. When they perch, however, they can be easily mistaken for moths. Common Checkered-Skippers are one of the few butterflies that rest with their wings drawn back like a moth, instead of holding them upright like most butterflies. But Common Checkered-Skippers are active during the day, when most moths are not.

Male Common Checkered-Skippers often fly back and forth, patrolling an area for females. In late afternoon males sometimes perch on a tall plant, but they will dart out to inspect anything that comes near.

Common Checkered-Skippers live throughout the year in the South. Each spring large numbers move northward. They feed on a wide variety of plants and may be the most common skipper in North America.

Did You Know?
- Common Checkered-Skipper caterpillars make folded-leaf nests in which they live and feed. Fully grown caterpillars hibernate over winter.
- Common Checkered-Skippers cannot survive very cold winters and may not be permanent residents in the North.

COMMON CHECKERED-SKIPPER

Large
white spots

Pale gray
underneath

**Female is black and white.
Male is more bluish gray.**

Habitat Common Checkered-Skippers are found in open, sunny places with low vegetation and some bare soil, including prairies, meadows, fields, roadsides, landfills, yards, gardens, and pastures. They range throughout most of the United States and as far north as central Canada and southern New England.

Favorite Plants Common Checkered-Skipper caterpillars can be found on mallows, hollyhock, and velvetleaf. Adult butterflies sip nectar from plants with white flowers, including asters and fleabane, red clover, knapweed, and many others.

When to See Them Adult butterflies can be found all year in the South. They can be seen throughout most of the North from March to September.